For Rent

For Rent

◆

Building Our Future Through Investment Properties

Jack Murphy
Lia Murphy

iUniverse, Inc.
New York Lincoln Shanghai

For Rent
Building Our Future Through Investment Properties

iUniverse books may be ordered through booksellers or by contacting:

iUniverse
2021 Pine Lake Road, Suite 100
Lincoln, NE 68512
www.iuniverse.com
1-800-Authors (1-800-288-4677)

Because of the dynamic nature of the Internet, any Web addresses or links contained in this book may have changed since publication and may no longer be valid.

The information, ideas, and suggestions in this book are not intended to render professional advice. Before following any suggestions contained in this book, you should consult your personal accountant or other financial advisor. Neither the author nor the publisher shall be liable or responsible for any loss or damage allegedly arising as a consequence of your use or application of any information or suggestions in this book.

ISBN: 978-0-595-46638-2 (pbk)
ISBN: 978-0-595-90933-9 (ebk)

Printed in the United States of America

Contents

Part V Protect, Preserve and Maintain

Part VI Dealing with Tenants

Part VII Conclusion

Acknowledgments

To our real estate agents and friends Patrick Abbott and Chris Brown, we thank you for your dedication and guidance to help us make the right decisions at the right time. We appreciate all that our lenders, Maria Labie and Tim Siwicki, and our accountant, Troy Barcume, have done to provide us with sound financial advice. We would like to thank our all-around handy man, John Rodriquez, who has ensured that the houses we buy stay standing and in great condition, without killing our budget. Our heartfelt thanks go to our parents Linda and Len Borek, and Jack and Jane Murphy for their support and encouragement throughout the entire transition and adventure. Finally, we must acknowledge our three young children who sat patiently in the car night after night while their crazy and obsessed parents drove all over God's half acre looking at land and houses.

Preface

We lived in Los Angeles for 12 years and during that time we often wrestled with the idea of getting into real estate. We had no desire to become licensed real estate agents mind you; we wanted to be landlords. We wanted to own property and have tenants pay our monthly mortgage payments for us. Our objective was to create a plan not only for short-term growth, but a potential long-term investment vehicle to pass on to our children.

Parents always wonder what their children will do when they get older and enter the job market. In the back of our minds, if we were to be diligent and stick to the primary goal, we could at the very least pass along to our kids a career option of investing and managing rental properties.

Our initial plan was really quite simple. We wanted to buy several houses over a period of time, using traditional financing as well as creative financing for the loans. These would initially be purchased at low prices and then rented out to tenants. We would keep the homes for years, and perhaps one day, the rent or the sale of the house would pay the college tuition for our children. Another possibility would be to use the income from these houses as an alternate resource for retirement money. The choice would be ours at some point in the future, but we were sure that this was the way to go.

We are both extremely fortunate to have great careers that we enjoy very much. Lia works for one of the top entertainment studios in California and Jack works in sales for a National Title and escrow company, also based in California. As many people might agree, there is an underlying fear of an unknown future. What if we were to lose our jobs? What if there was an unseen event that would cause one or both of us to be laid off, fired or unemployed? What would happen to our kids, our house and everything we had worked so hard to build over the years? We needed a stable and effective back-up income-generating plan that would provide us with choices, whether it was for emergencies, a rainy day fund, or a dream vacation around the world. Basically we wanted to create the ultimate financial security plan for ourselves and our family's future.

We had a little money saved and a little bit more in stocks and options that we would have access to if needed. But we were unsure how much we would need and even how to begin. On some days, even at the start of the 21st century when

California real estate was booming, we questioned whether or not real estate investing was a sound financial opportunity.

Occasionally we would discuss the possibility of opening up our own business. As an example, after shopping a wide variety of upscale clothing boutiques in LA, we considered opening up an alternative clothing store in a small Midwest town. The idea was to find a location in that quant little town's historic downtown area, right on main street for maximum store-front exposure and foot traffic. However, Lia was much more resistant to that. Statistically, small businesses have a difficult chance of succeeding and if they do, the owners struggle for years and years. Perhaps even more important, something like that was a full-time gig. It is not something we could do on the side with little or no stress. Owning and operating a store like that would require time, money and a commitment we were not yet prepared to give.

Every time we sat around the table and discussed what to do, we kept coming back to the same thing. Our best opportunity was to invest our money and time in real estate for long-term financial security and growth. Most of the people we knew who had money and solid wealth had achieved it via real estate, be it through appreciation of their primary home or by acquiring rental properties.

We read everything we could find on the subject of real estate as we were complete novices. Some of the books we read dealt with topics such as buying and renting homes, buying with no money down, and profiting from rent-to-own houses. Others told us how to flip homes, purchasing houses at a low price, then renovating them and selling them at a profit. Eventually we settled on a plan to be conservative investors which seemed to have the best chance for long-term success. We wanted to buy, rent and hold.

This book is the story of how we sold our primary home in California and moved across country to buy five homes, find tenants for our houses, and rent them out for a profit. All of this was accomplished while maintaining our current jobs and balancing our family life with careers.

Please understand that this is by no means a get-rich-quick book. This is a real-life example of two parents who discovered prudent and effective ways to buy, rent and hold properties for the long haul. It is also our personal experience at the very start of this adventure, including successes and failures as we continue with our endeavor.

Part I
A Jump Start

1

The Right Time

One early morning in the summer of 2006, Jack received a phone call from our real estate agent and very good friend in Santa Clarita, California, Pat Abbott. He asked what Jack was doing for lunch that day and if he would be available to meet with him. While Jack will always jump at the chance for a free meal, he was particularly intrigued by the curiously animated tone of Pat's voice. What could possibly be on his mind?

When they met at the restaurant, Jack noticed that Pat was a little extra happy. He always had a bounce in his step and was an all-around happy guy, but that day his grin seemed wider and his natural exuberance even more infectious. With his multitude of bright Hawaiian shirts, one's first impression of Pat might be that he would be more at home on the beach than in an office. This appearance however, is misleading, as he is more knowledgeable and experienced in real estate than his tops are colorful.

They started with small talk about how the families were doing, how the kids were and of course the weather, which was as hot as an oven outside thanks to the intense summer sun. After the small talk subsided, Pat broached the subject he had called to discuss.

"Are you and Lia still considering moving back to Michigan some day?" Pat asked.

Jack was now very curious as to why Pat would bring this up and why make a lunch date to ask that question. He is not the type of agent who would entice people to buy or sell a property so he can make a little more money. Pat is extremely successful and we oftentimes believe that the main reason he still sells houses is because he truly enjoys playing the game and sharing his wisdom along the way.

"Well Pat, as you know it's something we've tossed about the past few years. Most of our extended family still lives in Michigan and with our third child on the way, we realize that we would love to raise our children where we grew up.

But we're torn. We love California and after living in Santa Clarita for almost 13 years, this is home. Why do you ask?"

Pat chuckled slightly. "You're just not going to believe it."

"Believe what?" Jack asked.

"We've sold it."

"Sold what?"

Pat grinned. "SCV Homes."

"You're kidding!"

"Not about this. The time was right." Pat explained how he and his partners decided to sell their local and very successful real estate business to a large reality company.

"But that's not all. I moved the family and sold everything in California. We've left the state for the other coast." Pat had sold his big and expensive estate in Santa Clarita, his entire cache of rentals houses and all of his other property in Southern California and he had bought a home in South Carolina. He and his family had already moved there and the kids were already in South Carolina schools.

Jack was sure his jaw hit the floor boards. As he stared mutely at Pat, he asked the only thing he was able to mutter in his disbelief. "Why?"

Pat continued. "I'm convinced the real estate market here in Southern California is extremely super-heated. So much so that there just has to be a massive correction, one that would rival that seen in the late 80's and early 90's."

He continued by saying the dramatic increase in prices the past few years simply could not continue, especially when most of the residents of this state are not able to afford a place to live.

"So what does this mean for me and my family?" Jack asked.

"Time is running out … fast. If you're seriously considering moving out of the state, and cashing out on your equity, do it now."

Pat also had a handle of the real estate market throughout the country, including Michigan. He was a student of the industry, and he explained further.

"You paid $475,000 for your current house. The value is probably around $700,000 but that is not a guarantee. For that same purchase price, you could buy a home in Michigan that's almost double the size on an acre of land, easily."

"Wow. We could really lower our mortgage payments, which would almost make up for the freezing winters."

"That's a possibility, but here's another thought. What about rental properties … in Michigan?"

Rental properties were something we had thought about, but it just wasn't possible in Los Angeles or southern California. The numbers simply could not work due to the high home costs, high taxes and lower-than-needed rents. The risk in Southern California was greater than we were willing or able to undertake on our own. The financial stakes were much too high.

"Now's the time, Jack. If you want to move your family back to Michigan, this is your chance to put your house on the market, take the profits and run. Consider it your opportunity to take your winnings out of the new and improved California real estate lottery."

After lunch, Jack got in the car and immediately grabbed his cell phone to call Lia. He was convinced Pat was right, especially since he had sold everything and made such a drastic life change for his family. He also saw the beginnings of what Pat explained. It was true that they could have sold their house the year before at a higher price, maybe not much higher, but enough that told him it truly was the right time.

Lia would be a different audience, however. While she also wanted to move back to Michigan someday, there was always something that held her back: her career, the children, the weather, something. He would have to pull out all of the stops and do his best sales presentation ever.

"Lia, you'll never believe it. Pat has sold everything: his house, his business, all of the rental properties. He now owns nothing in California."

She also was stunned that he had sold everything and moved out of state. She wondered how much of it was a true prediction of what might happen, or was it nothing more then a gut feeling and a hunch. And frankly that is what it felt like it was, nothing but a big "you better be right" hunch. Would we stake our entire financial future on nothing more then someone else's forecast? Yank our kids out of the schools and day cares that they loved and we trusted and move 2500 miles away and start a new life all on someone else's bet? What about our friends and loved ones in Santa Clarita? Were we ready to leave all of that behind? Nobody ever visits Michigan on their annual vacations except people who are originally from Michigan and they only go back during the holidays to see their families. This could possibly be the last we would ever see people we had come to know and love ever again.

Later that night after dinner as we watched our two preschoolers running around our backyard, we discussed the conversation and news about Pat. We were still quite shocked that he had just sold everything, including the business, and moved his entire family to South Carolina in what appeared to be such a short time frame.

Lia's first question was, "Why South Carolina?"

Pat said he liked the weather a great deal there and also stated that the real estate market was much more favorable to that of California or other parts of the country.

We also discussed whether he was right or wrong from virtually every angle. Pat was usually right more often then he was wrong when it came to real estate. Our personal experiences with him led us to believe he would not do something as aggressive as that without a solid belief. But still, was he just blowing smoke for the first time, or was he right on the money and if so, should and could we listen to his advice?

2

Now What?

As we discussed Pat's move, we took all of this previous information into consideration. Were we actually seeing a market correction? Or was this just a blip on the real estate radar screen? These were very important questions for us as we had several issues to contemplate.

The obvious ones were the thought of selling our house in California and moving across country with two young children. On top of that, however, Lia was seven months pregnant with our third child. So we would also need to find the right time to move a new family of five and locate the right house for us which would most likely need to be done from afar. What about doctors, schools and daycare, and oh, we couldn't forget about finding new jobs somewhere along the way, too? And these questions would be considered easy ones if any of us or the new baby had any health concerns to think about. Yes, it was daunting on so many levels. But we couldn't shake the fact that there were other factors that made us believe that this was truly the right time for us.

In 2003, we purchased our house in Santa Clarita for $475,000. That was the listing price, the sellers were not interested in negotiating, and most sellers received multiple offers on their homes at that time. You either paid what they were asking for the house, and in many cases more then they were asking for, or you didn't get the house. The market was super-heated and you could basically watch your house value appreciate daily like you could monitor your electric meter. It was an amazing time to own a home in California. It felt like you had this magical bank in which money really did grow on trees and could be placed in your account.

By the late summer of 2005, the value of our home had skyrocketed to almost $750,000. While it was relatively new having been built in 2000, it was nothing extraordinary or truthfully deserving of a price that high. It was a single-story home with 4 bedrooms, 2 baths on a 10,000 square foot lot. Yes, the backyard was lush and beautiful with an outside living area and a water feature, but we had no basement. It was just strange to think that our comfortable yet modest house would be worth that much. So in our mind the house was over-valued due to demand. However, little did we know at the time that the Los Angeles real estate market was just about at its peak.

We had no plans of a permanent move in 2005, so we refinanced the house that summer, took out a little equity and bought a new RV so we could quench our wanderlust by touring the country. Luckily at that time we were conservative with this and we did not cash in anywhere near the appraised value. We knew in our hearts that $750,000 could not be maintained forever. Still, the houses in Santa Clarita were selling faster then you could put up the for sale signs. In fact, we did not even need to put up a sign when we decided to sell our previous house. That's how strong the market was in 2003. In those heady days of real estate bliss, offers came in before your house even hit the multiple listing services.

Yet this entire opportunity felt like it was more then just sell, move, buy and be really happy. Yes, it had the potential to be one big massive pain in the neck. If we were wrong, it could cost us everything we had worked so hard for years and years to obtain; it most likely would even cost us our jobs. At the same time, it could spell a bright new interesting and financially rewarding future.

We truly had thought about moving back to Michigan one day but there were so many reasons why it was easy to stay put. We had, however, always said that if we had a third child or if our house ever hit a certain price point, or if Lia had reached a certain point in her career, then we would move back home.

So after a few weeks of debate and after much involvement, coaxing and encouragement from our friends and parents, we decided to do it. We had looked online at homes for sale in Michigan and decided that this was it and the time was now. The prices in Michigan were at record lows. This was the chance we had hoped for: sell the house in California, buy a house in Michigan and also buy rental properties in Michigan if we had any profit from the California house sale. The market was perfect in Michigan for what we wanted to do. We were going to take the risk since we did have large loving families on both sides to welcome us. The long term reward was too great and the desire to have our kids growing up in the Midwest with their relatives close by greatly out weighed the fear-of-change concerns.

3

Making the Sale

Our next step was putting the house in California for sale and on the market. One piece of advice Pat told us years ago is to sell your own house first before finding and placing an offer on your dream house. The reason for this is to help ensure you are both financially and mentally able to negotiate intelligently as both a seller and a buyer. If you find that dream house first, your heart may make you do whatever you need to to sell your current home. This is extremely valuable advice! We learned this from the sale of our very first house when our initial buyers fell through at the very end of escrow and we know what it's like when you absolutely must have that house!

We had no idea how long it could take to show and sell our house. Past results were surely not indicative of any future events in this case by a long shot. It could take one day or it may take a year or more. It was the summer of 2006 and by now the homes were sitting on the market for quite a while: 30–60 days was not unheard of at this point. Some in our own neighborhood, roughly the same size as ours, had been on the market for longer then even that with little or no activity.

We looked closely at the homes for sale nearby as well as within about 10 miles of our place to get a general idea of what was on the market and what sold. If in fact the re-sale market was going down, and it was, then the homes for sale in our neighborhood were priced as if the market was still going up. We figured that that is why they were all still for sale. These people did not have a good agent nor were they receiving good advice. Or worse yet, they didn't listen to the good advice because they didn't like the numbers.

Everyone thinks their house is worth more than it is worth. We were no exception. There is nothing wrong with that from a "feel good" stand point, except when it comes time to sell it. We recall the debates we had when discussing the sales price. We both aimed way too high initially, but after proper research and thinking clearly, we knew what we needed to get out of it, so that gave us our financial window to work within.

We met with Pat to set the price, he recommended that we start off at $719,000 and see what happens. Though this seemed extremely high, he wanted to test the market and its volatility. To walk away with enough money to do what we wanted to do, our bottom price was no less then $640,000 so Pat felt $719,000 was a good initial price.

Within 3 days we had an interested couple who placed an offer on our house. Now that might seem amazingly fast, almost like it was too good to be true. And it was. Their offer was contingent upon them selling their condo, which they had yet to place on the market. After reviewing the comps for their condo, we felt their asking price was too high—they actually wanted more than the price of our house—so we asked them to drop their sales price. This would make for a quicker sale on their end and thus a faster sale on our end. They declined our advice and then interestingly stated that they thought we were asking way too much for our house anyway!

We didn't know whether to laugh or take it as an insult. After all, they had made an offer to us based on that particular sales price didn't they? Granted, their offer was for $690,000, but at the time, they made no other comments about our $719,000 list price. That said, we learned a good and a fast lesson: we were over-priced, especially if we were serious sellers who wanted to sell our home quickly.

The next day, we declined their offer and placed the house back on the market at a new lower price of $690,000. Yes, we dropped the price $30,000 in under a week, but we did not advertise it that way. Within a day, we had someone interested in looking at our house. They looked at it again the following night and we soon received an offer from them. They proposed $660,000, contingent upon the sale of their condo, and the good news was that their condo was already in escrow.

We countered at $665,000 with a two-month rent-back so we could at least have the baby with Lia's current doctor and at the hospital where our other two children were born. This would also allow us to have enough time afterwards in the event of any unplanned surprises and emergencies with our newborn. If they would accept that, we were also willing to throw in our patio furniture and out-door appliances that were easily worth thousands of dollars. As much as we liked them, they were more suited for the California climate and not for the harsh Michigan winters. They happily accepted our counter offer almost immediately, and we have been on friendly terms with the buyers ever since.

Part II
Finding Houses

1

A Home … Away from Home

Now that we had sold the California house, we needed to find a primary home for us to live all the way across the country in Michigan. We didn't have the time or money to hop on a plane and look at houses in person so we took advantage of the resources available to us on the internet and also asked our families to assist in our search.

Lia learned to master the real estate website, *realtor.com,* as well as many of the local agent's web sites. She quickly learned the lingo and what was meant by a "lovely view of the pond". View is the operative word here as there was often-times little backyard to speak of and limited access to that lovely pond. Custom paint often meant a horrific color that would inspire indigestion when you had dinner guests tour the house.

Fortunately, we also had local scouts that could help provide a trustworthy perspective of our potential new home. Initially Lia's family drove around pro-spective neighborhoods and sent us a list of homes for sale. From there, we inves-tigated those locations even further as we researched as many details as possible from the square footage and upgrades to the local elementary school. We also located other homes through these sources and began to narrow down the selec-tion.

Lia's Dad is retired and after we identified our top choices we asked him to drive by the homes, provide his thoughts on the house, yard and neighborhood, and possibly take a picture or two. Once we had narrowed it down to under 5 houses, we sent in our agent with our Dad. The hired gun was our Michigan real estate agent, Chris Brown. Like Pat in California, when Chris negotiated, he was in control. We didn't send in Chris until we really wanted more information or wanted to move the process to the negotiating stage.

After a few weeks we had narrowed it down to two houses. Chris had already spoken with the sellers' agents as well as the owners of both homes, so at this point we were ready to choose. We decided on the newest and largest one, that also boasted a one acre lot in a pristine neighborhood. When the house was first put up on the market, it was originally listed for sale at $560,000. It had dropped to $490,000 less than a year later and it was now sitting at the nice price of $475,000. You couldn't build that house for less then that. We wanted the house badly due to its beauty, size and location and had a pretty good feeling that it was at a really good price.

Chris slowed us down and kept reminding us over and over that we were in the driver's seat and to take our time and be patient. However, we didn't want to risk losing the home due to a weak initial low ball offer or by waiting too long to make an offer at all. You see, we actually were bit by that 'dream house' bug Pat had warned us about. Besides, coming from California we were actually afraid that somebody might be right in line after us! We actually did need a home at this point and we certainly didn't want to move to Michigan at the start of winter and have to live in a hotel with three kids, one of which was a newborn.

We decided to make a good solid one-time offer, still less than the asking price but not insultingly less. In our minds it was a strong and acceptable offer, we were not offering less to insult them, but to make our stand on one price and see what happens. So our offer was a take it or leave it one of $466,000, no contingencies, no nothing. They would even be allowed to stay in the house for one month for free while we were still living in California. We wanted to show them that while we were firm on our price, we did want to offer them something special. This was something that they would give them a small victory to make the deal more palatable. They said yes and we now had a place to live.

What We Learned

- Our advice to anyone who is buying their primary home or rental homes is to find a good qualified lender first. Talk to them. Find out what exactly you can qualify for and what that lender can do for you. Not all banks and lending institutions are the same. Not all loan officers are the same. Find someone you can work with over time and someone who can get the deal done and close to your terms. The lender with whom we were working with in Michigan was just outstanding. If it were not for her great skills and attention to detail, we never would have been able to get that deal done.

- Don't be stuck on fees when it comes to loans with your lender. Most fees are within reason, just check to make sure they are not too unreasonably high. The lender, notary and title and escrow companies have costs and these are people that deserve to be paid for their hard work and effort. Keep that in mind when doing your loans. No one likes to work with a borrower who says that they won't pay anyone anything for the work they do. If someone tells you they are doing it for free, be very weary of them, as not much in this world is free. I would rather know exactly what my lending team is making on my loans and frankly, I like them to make good money for honest work.

Remember the old saying: You get exactly what you pay for.

2

What a Find!

Now that we purchased our primary residence, Jack actually had the opportunity to see it live when he went to Michigan for a wedding while we still lived in California. That might be a bit backwards from the usual process, but we were thankful to at least have him see the house live before our move-in date!

Originally, the entire family was scheduled to see our niece get married in the quaint Bavarian town of Frankenmuth. Not only was our eldest daughter the Flower Girl, but our niece lived near us in Santa Clarita so we were especially close to her and her fiancé.

Just days before the purchase of our house in Michigan was final, our beautiful baby daughter was born happy and healthy. We were still living in California and would be for two more months. Unfortunately, our doctor felt the baby was much too young to fly (she would have been less than three weeks) so Lia and our two youngest children stayed behind. It was an adventure for Daddy and his eldest Daughter.

The objectives were to attend our niece's wedding, visit family and naturally go and see our new home. In addition, this would also allow John the chance to find neighborhoods for potential rental properties, the next phase in our plan. The idea was to tour as many cities and communities and see as many houses as possible in a short time. Jack needed to get a feel for the areas and the market. A friend once said that you need to see about five hundred houses before you find one you like. But, we were not buying our dream house this time; we were looking at houses as potential rental properties. They would have to be nice, in a clean and safe area and the monthly rent had to exceed the total amount of monthly out of pocket on our end.

We diligently targeted and reviewed the areas we thought looked good online before the trip to Michigan. We looked at houses in Saginaw, Flint, Romeo, St. Clair Shores and Royal Oak online. We decided that Jack would look around in Saginaw, sixty minutes north of our new house in Michigan and in and around the Romeo and Washington area. Both of these areas are within five minutes of our new house.

After a few days in town, Jack realized that Saginaw was too far to drive once a week to check on the tenants or the houses. In Romeo, the property taxes would simply erode any of our gains. He then did a quick search with the in-laws borrowing their car in the areas in and around Mt. Clemens, Michigan, which is about fifteen minutes from our new home. The prices there were in the range, but due to the neighborhoods being historical, any maintenance and updating would require input from City Hall which did not seem worth the hassle.

He had all but given up until they decided to leave a bit early for their flight back to California. During that drive, Jack asked his father in-law to try an area named Warren, Michigan. After driving up and down a few streets and seeing row after row of "For Sale" signs and many flyers, he started to get a strong feel for the area. Kids were playing outside; people were walking around or working on their houses. It seemed like a very comfortable family-friendly area with bungalow-style homes with prices between $40,000-$80,000. The neighborhood and houses were cute and well maintained. All we needed now was to get an idea of what the rents where like.

Once Jack had seen enough he told his father in-law that they could head to the airport. He had seen all he needed to see at this point and that it looked like the perfect area. Besides, our daughter was in the backseat and getting tired of looking at houses. She was ready for the five-hour flight back to California so she could see her Mom.

As they were heading out to the main road from the subdivision we noticed one last house for sale with flyers attached in an info-tube. They did one last stop and pulled the flyer. It was for sale for $59,000 and on that same flyer two other homes were listed that the sellers advertised as well. Those houses were listed at $65,000 and $55,000. One already had tenants and the rents were shown to be at $750 per month.

Well, now we not only had the answer to what rents were like in Warren, we had a glimpse at what our first three rental houses could be as well. Jack immediately called our agent, Chris, before the flight left from Detroit Metro Airport and told him what he discovered. He provided all of the pertinent contact information and asked him to get us the best deal. Jack had full faith that Chris would not only get us the best deal on these three houses, but that he would also make sure we were not inheriting someone else's problems.

What We Learned

In order to accomplish what we have, the most important thing we have learned to date is the importance of having a real estate agent that we could trust, one in whom we had the confidence we were told the truth at all times. Trust is paramount as many decisions were made based on sound and honest input by our agents.

- We had not only one trustworthy agent, but two. This saved us a lot of time and money as well as a ton of future headaches. Our agents taught us things that we would use later for purchase deals as well as on deals that fell apart. Both Pat and Chris welcomed the opportunity to help teach us the business.

- We had a great lender. Maria Labie with Citizens First Bank in Shelby Township, Michigan got the deals done. She was a very positive, effective and a wonderful communicator. Her mantra with us always was, "Just please trust me." We did, she treated us perfectly, and we never argued over the little things. We wanted her to be successful at her job, to be happy and positive, and we knew that if she was happy and happy with us, that she would go to bat for us with her underwriters if needed.

- We did our research before hitting the ground. We used the tools we had available online to explore virtually before we burned gas. We looked at hundreds of neighborhoods and homes online before anyone hit the pavement. Though people say it often, it is so true. "What did we do before the internet?" With today's technology you can view homes inside and out, map them, assess the school system, and check for sex offenders in the state and national registry. You can do all the research you need without ever leaving your desk. We bought our first four houses in Michigan basically site unseen. $650,000 in real estate purchases with out ever setting foot in the door of any of the homes. The combined values on all houses based on appraisals at this point of $750,000.

- We established and upheld the objectives for our rental properties. We discussed and agreed upon the long-term purpose of these homes and we made decisions based on our objectives. As stated, our goal is not to make a quick profit, but to buy, rent and hold for many years. As part of that we must ensure that rent is being paid, and that we have a positive cash flow as quickly as possible. The idea is to make each house self sufficient based on the renter making the rent payments.

- Finally, we have a financial plan, or as Jack likes to say, "We did the math." To meet our objectives we knew what the financial numbers had to be. Using online mortgage loan calculators, we were able to estimate mortgage payments for any size loan we would possibly consider. We never deviated from what we needed and what the plan was. For instance, we knew that a $55,000 house, with 10% down ($5,500) was going to have a monthly payment of around $350 with today's rates. We included projected taxes, which in our case usually run $1,000 per year as well as insurance at $500 per year. So the mortgage payment at $350 plus taxes and insurance at $125 was $475. We figured an additional $100 per month for maintenance and water bills for a grand total of $575.00 per month. So rent at $700 means a profit of $125 per month or $4,500 per year on 3 houses. Imagine that on 10, 15 or 20 homes? Plus, there is a nice tax benefit for which you may qualify.

One final note here: Tax laws vary and change from time to time, so check with your financial advisor to see if you would qualify for special tax breaks on rental properties.

Part III
Making it Work

1

The Money

When buying rental houses, you need to be sure the money works in your favor. What we mean by this is that you simply must bring in equal to or more then what you spend. Preferably, you should strive to bring in more. Also, it is very important to know what the property taxes or other community fees are on a particular property before you make an offer. High property taxes could wipe out your profit and make an initially good deal a bad one.

We figured that with the rents hovering around $650-$850 in the Warren, Michigan area, we could only afford to buy houses in the $50,000-$65,000 range. This would mean a total mortgage payment with taxes and insurance of close to $500 per month, fortunately there were a great deal of houses in Warren at those prices, and many of those seemed like they might be potential properties for us to consider. But this is where it is important to do a thorough inspection of the house for any hidden disasters just waiting for the next owner.

Like we said earlier, it takes a lot of searching to find the right place. We figured that we saw almost one thousand homes online and in person before Jack stumbled upon the three that were being sold by one seller. It wasn't just sheer luck, it was looking and looking and not jumping at the first things that seemed promising. And trust us, there were many that at the time and since then have looked good to us only to find out later in the process that they were total disasters or disasters waiting to happen.

We recall one time while on a house inspection with our trusty house inspector. The house was in such disrepair that we could only feel sorry for the tenants. The sink was leaking so badly in the kitchen that the bucket under the pipe was overflowing and the water was running throughout the kitchen. The power outlets in the kitchen and in the bathroom didn't work due to blown fuses. So, we stopped the inspection, Jack went out to the truck, got pliers and fuses and the inspector and Jack fixed the leak and got all the outlets working properly. This is something their landlord should have done a long time ago for these folks. This is an example of how we do not want to act.

The same tenants said the heat didn't blow out very well and the system seemed to be under some strain. We pulled the filter and noticed that it was so old it was actually covered in a greasy slimy gooey mixture. We cleaned it out as best we could and fired up the heater. Almost instantly, nice fresh hot air was blowing throughout the house to the sheer joy of the tenants. It was February and quite literally it was freezing cold outside.

When the tenant asked if we were buying the house and how happy she was that we were going to be the new landlords, we had to tell her that was probably not going to happen due to some personal issues that had arisen. We didn't have the heart to tell her that if all these little things were wrong, we were quite frankly petrified of what we couldn't see. Afterwards, Jack and the inspector discussed their review of the house and came to the instant conclusion that the seller was trying to unload major problems and that this was a big time "Pass."

As mentioned, remember to do the math before you buy a house to rent out. We cannot stress this enough and often enough. It's not that difficult and a little preparation can save you a ton of grief later on when an unexpected tax bill or water bill arrives. Don't be afraid to spend a little time and energy now to save a lot later.

EXAMPLE OF A SIMPLE DEAL

Mortgage

Purchase price:	$50,000
Down payment:	$ 5,000
Loan amount:	$45,000
Interest rate:	7.5%
Total base monthly payment:	$315.00 per month for 30 years

Real estate property taxes due annually
$1,200 per year or $100 per month set aside

Homeowners Insurance
$500 per year or $42 each month set aside

Monthly Payments

Mortgage:	$315
Property Taxes	$100
Insurance	$ 42
	$457

Incidentals
We suggest adding an additional amount, possibly $100, for basic home repairs or other utilities you may decide to cover. Please note, however, that emergencies will occur so you should also have additional funds set aside for those unexpected occurrences.

Your Grand Total:	**$557** per month
Analysis	$700 per month
Monthly Rental Fee:	-$557
Net income	$143

Keep in mind, that you are making $143 per month while your tenant is making your mortgage payment. Basically someone else is using their money to do your savings. $143 each month may not seem like too much since it may take almost three years at that rate to pay off your down payment, but hopefully during this time this house will be building its equity while you, in turn, are decreasing the amount you owe on the house.

On top of all of this is the year end financial gain you can receive on your taxes. Please consult a tax advisor to see if and how you can benefit. This is why we believe owning rental properties is indeed a long-term proposition

2

Finding Tenants

Almost every single book that we have read on the subject of renters gave this advice when interviewing tenants: screen, screen and when you feel like you have done your homework on them, screen them all over again. With their approval, run credit reports, call employers and previous landlords and get personal references. Do Google searches and background checks. Do everything you can to limit your risk and the risk to your house.

This is all great advice, particularly for first-timers like ourselves, and we do believe the guidance is valid and appropriate. However, we did not initially expect what an impact "the human factor" would have on us. We discovered that the soft spots in our hearts speak to us quite loudly.

We have given people an opportunity to rent a house from us when others might not have. We have not done rigorous background checks on all our current tenants because there have been times when we felt it more important for a family to have a house during the cold winter months versus having them wait for the paperwork to be completed. Do we recommend this for everyone? Absolutely not, but we know it is important to share this because it has taught us valuable lessons and allowed us to set the guidelines for our tenants even more clearly.

Yes, this has back-fired on us, twice already in the past year. However, it has worked well on two other occasions. In all cases, we accept and have learned from the initial decisions that we made. We like to believe we're trying to help people going through tough times, whether they appreciate it or not. We're certainly more cautious going forward, but we are willing to negotiate and understand the situations potential tenants may find themselves.

We have one house that has a Section 8 tenant. This is a type of federal assistance program provided by the United States Department of Housing and Urban Development (HUD) that is dedicated to sponsoring subsidized housing for low-income families and individuals. Section 8 actually refers to the specific portion of the U.S. Housing Act in which the program is authorized.

The tenant is a great guy who was shot in the head several years ago by gang members while he was waiting for his school bus. Because of this horrific crime, he is not able to work. The Section 8 program pays the majority of his rent and allows him to live on his own. From a landlord's perspective, this program is extremely satisfying as we have the government's commitment that we will have a tenant for a certain period of time and the checks are automatically deposited into our back account at the start every month.

Section 8 qualification as a landlord is pretty easy too. You simply put your house for rent with "Section 8 Accepted" written somewhere, and then when you find a Section 8 tenant to fill the vacancy. Most prospective tenants will tell you immediately if they are Section 8 and they will ask if you accept Section 8 tenants. The tenant then works with you and the government to make the rent dollar amount work. In some cases the tenant may have to come up with a little extra themselves each month, but in most cases the program covers the entire thing.

The thing to remember here is that as part of the Section 8 program, an inspection is required before any paperwork is signed and agreed to and that process can take anywhere from thirty to sixty days. Be prepared and make sure you know what Section 8 requires you to provide for the tenant with respect to things such as appliances and décor as well as general updates to the home.

The Section 8 program also runs periodic inspections of the house as will many cities or municipalities. Sometimes, you will have to pay for these inspections, so be prepared for this cost. For our house in Warren, it's usually only a hundred dollars every few years.

Here is what we do when we rent out a house. First, we no longer place ads in the paper as they cost too much money. We did it once and for the three hundred bucks we had one hundred phone calls with zero visits to view the place. Now we have learned to place a "For Rent" sign out in front of the home, with an information tube full of the property profile sheets. Each sheet has a clear and concise explanation of the house, the square footage, monthly rent and total move-in costs. This helps provide most of the answers for anyone who may be interested in the house.

By doing this, we typically have received at least five calls per day. Once we had to go back to the house the next day and take the sign down because we had so many calls. Now we realize that this might not happen in every neighborhood, but Warren is a relatively large suburb adjacent to the city of Detroit. This is also a neighborhood that has a lot of rental properties and our houses are located off a busy thoroughfare. So we know that there are a lot of people driving up and down these streets looking for a potential home to rent, just as we drove around seeking homes to buy.

If any prospective tenant is interested in seeing the house after we've discussed the terms over the phone, we will arrange a visit. From there, if they continue to express interest we ask them to complete an application form. We don't take a credit application nor do we complete a background check. We tell them what we expect from them and what they can expect from us. Jack will usually sit and talk with them at great length. They learn about us and he learns about them.

For us, this has been a great way to help screen tenants. He tells them that what they are undertaking is a business agreement. They pay us, we pay the bank and we all get to keep the house. If they don't pay us, we can't pay the bank and the house is taken away from both of us.

We do offer our tenants a five-day grace period on their rent. We recognize that people have different pay schedules and since most tenants send us their check, this allows them those few extra days for the mail to reach us.

We also request that they contact us immediately if they are having a problem and are going to be late with rent or the payment is going to be short. We do not want them to be afraid to pick up the phone or to avoid our calls if rent is a few days late. There is usually a way to work around these situations and the more we know the better off the situation will be. If Jack calls and no one responds or calls him back, then we expect the worst. However, if they call us first to ask for an extension then we will usually honor that request. We want an open line of communication with our tenants and if we can work out a situation that works for us all, we will all sleep better at night.

We also don't want to be looking for tenants all the time and we tell our new tenants that each time. We also offer them a payment plan. Pay the first half on the first of each month and the other half on the fifteenth. This oftentimes works for people if this syncs up with their paycheck schedule. We also have a program for people who may have difficulties coming up with the 1–1/2 month security deposit. We allow our new tenants the opportunity to spread the security deposit over a 3-month time frame.

This process has helped us lock down tenants fast, but it also can be more difficult to weed out the deadbeats. We will share more about our personal experiences with difficult tenants in an upcoming chapter.

We have had two tenants in a row that have been just great. They keep their houses in great condition and pay on time every single month without fail. These tenants have been grateful to us for not taking their past problems into account. We have told them that we don't care as much about what they did in the past, this is their chance to move forward in a positive direction. Yes, this is a business agreement and we cannot stress that enough to our tenants. Nothing is personal, it's business, but they are examples of strong partnerships.

The last thing here we want to address is how we treat our tenants. We try to leave them alone and while we drive by the houses regularly, it is at most once a week or two and we do so during the day or the early evening. We do not want them to feel as though we're constantly checking up on them and we definitely never send workers out to the houses without first obtaining the tenants permission. We act as if it is their house and try to instill in them pride of ownership so to speak. We want them to respect us so they in turn respect our houses. Treat people how you yourself want to be treated: the golden rule!

Again, we need this to work for them so it works for us. We don't want to be looking for tenants every other month. We want to be out looking for new opportunities and investments.

Part IV
A Different Kind of Real Estate Deal

1

The Next Good Find

Once we had acquired a few rental houses we were ready for more. We had been bitten by the bug but we needed to find the right deal. We had made offers on a few houses since our initial house purchases, but problems arose during inspections that turned us away. We wanted the deal that felt right with a really good house we were confident we could rent. We were now ready to be a little pickier.

What did we learn on the houses we didn't buy? One of the most important things is that it pays to have a home inspection. It costs only a couple hundred dollars and is worth every penny. Yes, we have spent money just to say no, but we would rather spend a little now then a lot later.

On each of the houses we bought, we had the seller pay for a one year home warranty through escrow. This has saved us a lot of money, especially on our homes that are over fifty years old. The furnace went out in one house and the electric shorted out on another. On another house we added an appliance warranty to the electric bill with Detroit Edison that we pay for separately. It's cheaper to pay $200 a year to warranty the major appliances in a fifty-year-old house than it is to replace one major appliance per year. We are firm believers in insurance protection. In the case of rental houses, if it can go wrong, it probably will. We have done well to remember that we are not there inside the house daily to care and maintain for the appliances and the house ourselves. Someone who doesn't own the house is doing this for us. Of course, be sure to include any additional warranties in your financial plan.

As we stated, we were ready for the next big deal. It needed to be right. We had scoured real estate websites daily and we were just coming up with much of the same. We wanted something different. We wanted to buy a house with as little down as possible in a nice clean area. But it still had to fit in our master plan and fall within our parameters and we just were not finding many that fit or felt right.

We drove around and looked at houses and checked the local newspapers "For Sale" sections daily. Then one Saturday morning we saw an ad for a house for sale by owner, $65,000, Land Contract terms with $5,000 down. The city was Inkster, Michigan. This was a little over an hour from our house, but it was near the airport so we decided that it might just be a gem.

On rental houses, or Non-owner-occupied properties as they are called, most lenders these days want at least 10 percent down. At $5,000 this deal was only about 7.5 percent and we had a plan that we could get the whole deal refinanced later with a bank for a grand total of roughly 10 percent including all closing costs.

Jack immediately called the seller and got the address for a drive-by. We loaded up the kids in the car and headed out to see this potential new purchase. It was a cute 3 bedroom, 1 bathroom, white house with black window edging. It had a nice-sized yard, it was clean and well kept and it was on a street that had several kids out playing. We got out, took a long look at the house, and decided it was exactly what we wanted.

Just about that time the seller called and said he was on his way and would we wait for him. When he showed up we looked at the inside and did a quick assessment of the place. On the inside he pointed out the new carpet, new shades, new paint and all brand-new appliances purchased a few months earlier. The place was in great condition. Our initial guess was that it would appraise for $70,000 or so easily, and it ended up appraising for $75,000.

We told him right then and there that we would buy it for $5,000 down, 30 years on a land contract for $65,000. He initially stalled at the 30 years, but we informed him that we planned on refinancing the purchase as soon as possible. We felt that at most we would make payments for a year, but that we needed terms that kept our payments low initially so we could get a renter in it and make money. Plus, we advised him that we were not haggling with him over the price so he had a small initial victory. The seller agreed with our offer and two days later we had a renter put a deposit on the place and all ready to move in to the house!

About 30 days later, after the land contract recorded with the county, we went back to our trusty lender and we refinanced, actually purchased it again in a way. Our total out of pocket was the lenders processing fees and title and escrow of $1,700 plus the $5,000 down we gave the seller. This was right about at the 10 percent we wanted to be at for this deal. We had a renter in the property paying us $700 per month, on a monthly PMTI (payment, mortgage and taxes) on our end of about $550.

We saved a bunch of fees on this deal, including any real estate agent commissions. This was not our initial intent, but it just worked out that way. Also as you start investing in rental properties or investment property, at some point your money might be tight and you will want to find a cheaper way to do a particular deal. At this stage, we needed a cheaper deal. Going through an agent for this deal would have cost us easily an additional $2,000 or more.

At this point, we now had $715,000 in loans on five houses with a combined appraised value over $825,000.

LAND CONTRACT: TIMELINE OF EVENTS

Saturday Morning—We saw an ad in the paper and went to see the property. We accepted the offer on-site but on our terms, and made arrangements to sign the land contract and pay the down payment Monday morning.

Monday morning—We met with the seller at his bank, completed the land contract and paid $5,000 down. We received the keys and went to our new house immediately after the purchase. Our monthly payment with taxes and insurance (PMTI) was $600 under the land contract terms that we negotiated. This was to be our payment for a very short time.

Wednesday Morning—We met with the prospective new tenant at the new home, signed the lease agreement, and received the deposit money. The tenant moved in the following week.

Thursday—We went to the County offices and recorded the land contract.

Friday—We went to the city of Inkster and had the water bill and the tax bill placed in our names. In the afternoon we had insurance placed in our names as well.

30 days later we refinanced the entire deal and bought out the land contract with a traditional bank mortgage loan. Our PMTI dropped to $500 per month on this deal after the refinance. This turned out to be our best deal so far as we also had immediate equity based on the value of the house.

2

What We Have Learned So Far

We have learned that buying houses is not that difficult. The key is to gain control of the property; in the previous example the land contract was a perfect vehicle for us at that time. Here is what else we have learned.

- It takes a little money to do this, but this is the safe and right way to invest in rental properties for middle income families in nice clean neighborhoods. Surely safer then buying with no money down and taking out all the perceived equity at closing. We have renters paying the mortgage, taxes and insurance for us on each house and we have retained all the equity so far on each property. Some day we may tap into it, but for now, we have equity if needed.

- Our plan is to hold on to our properties for the long term as investments, not to flip and make a quick buck. We remind ourselves this each and every time we look at a house or land that looks really cheap. We start thinking about buying and flipping but always come back to our original plan. With three young children and full-time careers outside this venture, we simply do not have the time to invest in refurbishing a house.

- We only buy houses in areas that we would live in if need be. We always tell our prospective tenants that if we ever lost our house, we would move into whichever rental house was available. That is also one of the reasons why we put money into them. We want them to look nice and be kept in good condition. It is a reflection of us as property owners and we want that to always be positive in our neighborhoods.

- It is O.K. to say "No" to a deal. We have turned down more houses then we have bought by a long shot.

- We have learned how to buy a house without a real estate agent and how at the same time to reduce our out of pocket costs greatly. That is money then saved for the next deal. It may not be appropriate on every deal, but for a land contract or seller-financed deal, it's perfect.

- There is a way to urge tenants out of the houses fast. We cannot afford to have any property sitting around vacant without people paying rent for any prolonged period of time. Time is money.

- It is possible to structure a land contract in our favor and negotiate the deal ourselves. We can be creative and assertive when making offers.

- It is imperative to treat people fairly and with dignity. Not all tenants are going to be perfect, but in most cases they are more than willing to leave when they can't pay rent as long as they are asked properly to do so. In some cases, you will come across the professional tenant who knows all the ins and outs and will try to milk you dry. We are weary, but we also don't treat everyone as if they are about to take advantage of us. If it happens then it happens. So far, we have been super lucky and have not had that tenant yet.

- When we treat people fairly and give them grace periods, they respond by keeping our houses clean and good condition. They fix the little things without even thinking about it. We respect them and in turn they respect us and respect our property.

- Just remember the time when you were a renter and all the things you said you would never do if given the chance to be a landlord. Now is the time to be that person. Make a difference and make someone happy. Your kindness will be returned to you.

3

Vacant Land

The thought had crossed our minds many times that maybe we should purchase vacant land while the prices were cheap. We could simply sit on it for years, possibly build if desired, but ultimately let the property appreciate.

We decided that this would be a nice addition to our portfolio and it was time to start looking seriously. We started driving all over the state of Michigan looking at lots and acres and all sorts of vacant land. We put an offer on one and then backed out immediately once we saw that 70 percent of the land was wet lands that the owner was trying to hide during the sale.

There was another property that was full of trees on a hill overlooking a large meadow. But when we unbuckled the entire family to walk around the lot we were immediately overrun by a swarm of mosquitoes and other unknown insects and we realized we weren't yet ready to fight nature just yet.

After a few months we decided that the best deals were in the northern part of Michigan, up near the top of the mitt but not as far north as the Upper Peninsula. We narrowed the search through extensive online research once again, and also via a few driving trips throughout the lower, mid and thumb part of the state. We would grab the kids and hop in the car for a Saturday drive and cover a large area just looking around and deciding thumbs up or down (no pun intended) on whether that part of Michigan was what we wanted. We didn't get out and walk land, we just drove around on the surface streets and tried to get a general idea of whether the area worked for us or not.

While perusing the local papers one Saturday morning we came across a potentially good deal and it was land only, no house. It was located just outside the northern Michigan town of Traverse City, a popular resort community on Lake Michigan. The ad listed a specific lot of 5 acres for $35,000.

This looked like a great deal and we felt this could be it. We packed the kids in the car once again, grabbed enough food for the journey and headed up north. It was a four-hour drive one way to the land. We had printed the directions to the property from the website as well as the brochure from the real estate agent/seller. We did not call the seller before we got in the car. We just decided to go and look and who knows, maybe along the way or once we got up there something else might come our way.

Once we reached the land, it was a fairly easy decision. We wanted it. It was located on a cul-de-sac after a nice drive down a beautiful tree-filled road. This lot was one of 10 already prepped lots for future home sites. Each lot was five acres and in beautiful shape. We could easily imagine bringing our RV there for a weekend trip or someday building a log home on the property. Jack then placed a call to the seller. After playing phone tag for about half an hour, we finally connected as we began our trip back home. At that point, with the whole family sound asleep in the car, he and Jack negotiated the deal to purchase the land.

The following Monday, we made a few calls and were able to track down financing and put a plan together. Because there were some discrepancies in the pricing on this property via the internet and the ad in the paper, Lia advised that we "negotiate" a lower price and some seller money too at closing. After talking to the loan officer at the bank, we had a plan in place.

We approached the seller with an offer of $1,500.00 down, on a 100 percent financed deal with a local bank in Traverse City, Michigan with the seller giving us 3 percent back at closing. Instead of $35,000 we offered $33,500. The seller give-back at closing basically ensured that we would have minimal if any out-of-pocket money at the end of the deal. It was a pretty sweet deal. And at the end of the day our monthly payment on this deal with the bank is about $250 per month on a 5-year ARM (adjustable rate mortgage) with taxes included.

Normally, when you buy vacant land you need at least 10 percent down. What we found through just a little research is that with our good credit and good mortgage payment history, going to a local bank in that area gave us the chance to buy the land with basically zero down. They wanted our business bad basically. And by striking a deal with the seller we had them cover our closing costs, which consisted of credit report fees, title and escrow fees and other miscellaneous lender fees.

All in all, we found that this deal was one of our best yet and most importantly it was by far the easiest to accomplish in the shortest period of time.

One of the things we did for the bank to make the approval process faster and easier was to provide them with everything they asked for and more. Not only did we give them what they wanted, we gave them other things like rental leases and rental history on all our existing properties. We put everything in folders and labeled them according to the content so it would be easier for the underwriter at the bank to find information and make a decision. As an example, they asked for all 401k information.

We printed off our most recent statements, the complete history including the amount deducted each week out of our paychecks. We labeled each one as to whose it was and then put them in a folder labeled 401k. We did this for everything they asked for. They asked for mortgage statements, we gave them the most recent statement plus a print out of the entire history of payments on that mortgage we just negotiated from the mortgage company.

You see, what we did was go above and beyond to make sure the lender and the underwriter knew and understood that we are serious and not slackers. This is business to us and we want everything perfect and in all cases we go above and beyond to prove to them that we are serious investors and good risks.

We must also note that since the time when we first wrote this book, the mortgage industry has undergone serious changes. Some of the deals we have discussed may not be possible in today's market.

Part V
Protect, Preserve and Maintain

1

Protect Yourself and Have a Good Team

In the society we live in today, anyone can sue you for pretty much any reason they want to if they and their attorney are hungry enough. Not that they will always win, but people out there are willing to try. Like we stated earlier, we believe in insurance protection. Spend a little now to save a lot later. There are several things we have done to help protect us.

First, once we had accumulated the 4 rental properties, we started a Limited Liability Corporation (LLC) to protect our personal assets from any yet to be named threat.

Setting up the corporation was quick and easy. We decided to use a company that specializes in setting them up and helping to manage them. Its initial cost was $250 dollars and then $125 per year. It was easy and they did all the work for us. And most importantly, it has given us peace of mind ever since.

You can set up your corporation or LLC yourself if you wish to save money, the same way you can do your own taxes to save money, but we prefer to be safe rather then have some loop hole come up at the wrong time that will cost us everything and ruin our future. Like legal matters and taxes, we like to have professionals do their job for us. The LLC was certainly no different in our minds.

Second, we strongly recommend that you find a good accountant. The tax benefits to owning and renting real estate are enormous for some people. We used to use a general tax preparation company for all our tax returns but once we started acquiring property and created the LLC, we felt we needed a much more knowledgeable accountant. A fee for tax advice and preparation is money well spent.

As you can see, what we have done is surround ourselves with a team. We have a real estate team for help, guidance and advice as well as showings. We have a lending team that is there to tell us what we can and can not do and what we need to get the deals done. We have an accountant who ensures that we are paying our taxes properly as well as getting credit for the deductions we desire and need as well as coordinate with the LLC to ensure total compliance and adherence to rules and guidelines.

Third, you should make sure you have an attorney that you can trust and call for advice. You may not need this person all that often, but when the time comes, an attorney is just like insurance. When you need him or her, you are glad that that person is on our team.

Fourth, get a good handy man. We prefer not to do the work on our properties ourselves. We like the work to be done right, be clean and be warranted if available. We may need to spend a little bit more now, but this may help ensure we don't spend a lot later to re-repair something.

Our handy man has saved us thousands of dollars and loads of time. He can do just about everything and does it for about a quarter of what anyone else would charge. He is not perfect, but he is close to perfect, he is cheap and he is always available to do repairs and improvements for us

By having professionals do the work they do best, we are then able to write off the materials and labor on our tax return for this business. If we do the work ourselves, based on how we operate the business, we can only write off the material and not the labor or time. We find it is more prudent to have someone else do it and we are rewarded with a better write off at tax time.

As with anything else tax related, please consult a qualified tax professional to see what is best for you.

Fifth, make sure all your insurance coverages are up-to-date and at the proper limits for liability. We add on the basic homeowners' policies by having home warranties on the new houses and on the older one we have the appliance service plan via the local utility company for just a few dollars a month. On top of all of that, we have a million dollar general liability policy that provides us with that last layer of protection. That only costs us a few hundred dollars per year but protects us on the rental home side as well as at our private residence and beyond.

In addition, stay involved and attune to the local news in your rental neighborhoods. It's important to know what is going on day to day around your houses. Remember, they are your houses and it is your neighborhood, you just don't happen to live there at the moment. We get the local newspaper for that community and that gives us all the local news in and around our rental houses. We know about their local politics, what's the day-to-day crime like and honestly, we always look to see if by some crazy chance something happens at one of our houses and it makes the news.

One day Jack decided to take a quick spur of the moment drive by our houses on a Sunday morning. When he arrived at one, the street was loaded with police cars and K-9 units. As he approached our house he could see our tenant seated in the back seat of one of the police cars. Apparently there was a domestic dispute and drugs were found. The police were very nice and explained the whole situation. They acted quite surprised that Jack was there.

Whenever you are in the area of your houses, drive by them. You don't need to stop by for a personal visit, but it's good for them to see you in the neighborhood. Jack loves to drive by the houses when the tenants are outside. They see him and he waves, but he keeps on driving. The tenants see that he may not call or bug them but that he is driving by the house simply to check in. This leaves them with the impression that he is approachable, just a phone call away and that he can be at the house in a moment or two.

2

Before the Offer

Prior to any financial commitment, we recommend that you interview a few lenders. Tell them that you are interested in buying rental properties and let them know everything about you and your purchase. They need to know about you personally too. You need to advise them of your credit worthiness and your past credit history with loans as well as your payment history. Be open, honest and upfront with them. Do not chance anything here as it could cost you deposit money and a strong, needed relationship.

One of the worst things you can do is find a house, make an offer and find out after the fact that you do not qualify for the loan you need. What we do, even on deals that fall apart, is ensure we have the approval upfront from our lender and make sure we have all the money necessary to complete the transaction. We then take the steps to make an offer contingent upon inspection and appraisal. A pre-approval letter for the exact sale amount, no more and no less, is a great sales tool all by itself.

Seven Sources of Money for the Down Payment and Loan

There are many ways to get the money necessary for the down payment on your rental homes. Sometimes you will need to be both creative and a good sales person. Each of these has risk and possible tax implications, so weigh each option carefully and check with your tax advisor before just jumping in head first. Keep in mind that all loans have interest rates and must be paid back. We personally have used profits from the sale of house, personal savings and cashed out of some stocks to buy our houses. Here is a list of seven potential sources for your down payment.

1. Take a home equity loan or a second mortgage from your current home

2. Refinance your primary house and take cash out to cover the deposit or even the entire purchase price of a rental home. "Be the bank" this way, and in most cases you can even write that loan off on your taxes too.

3. Use credit cards or credit card checks to cover the initial down payment, but check with your lender first to make sure your debt to income ratio will not be hurt by using this method. Please take into account the interest rate of your credit card as this could imbalance your financial plan.

4. Use your personal savings, stocks, bonds or stock options. Cash in savings bonds or government back securities if you have them.

5. If it's the purchase of your first primary home, you may have legal access to some of the funds within your 401k plan at work. Check your plan guidelines or your plan administrator.

6. Borrow money from relatives or friends; even bring them in on the deal to entice them to invest with you. If you choose this option, ensure your partnership is clear and possibly captured in writing.

7. Try to obtain a 100% or more financing loan. That can be difficult with rental properties, but somewhat easier with primary homes. Check with your lender and be aware that your credit worthiness is a major factor in the rate and terms of any loan.

Part VI
Dealing with Tenants

1

Fair Treatment

We offer our houses to anyone who meets our simple criteria: a tenant that likes the house, has a steady job and has the necessary income to meet the monthly rent payment. If these are met, we are usually willing to give it a try. After this, however, it oftentimes is a matter of first-come first-served.

This is one of the reasons why we use the information tube on our "For Rent" sign out front. First, this helps us by knowing that those people who do call are aware of the key details of the house, including the rent amount, the location, the size and the exterior design of the house. Second, this allows us to encourage a sense of urgency as we typically receive multiple interested parties and we are upfront about that fact when interviewing multiple candidates. We find that the people that make the concerted effort to be responsive, on time, dependable and honest in their initial dealings with us are indeed those that are the ones who end up signing the agreement.

At this point it is imperative that we remind you to never discriminate against anyone and to follow your State, Federal and City ordinances at all times. Being a landlord is an extremely important responsibility and conducting business in a respectable and legal way is a must.

Of course, hiccups do occur along the way. We have already had tenants who were identity thieves. If we had run a background check and been more thorough in our review of their application, we might never have agreed to have them sign the lease. But then again, this might have been difficult to determine since they were posing as other people! Fortunately, they did not stay in our house long and we only recognized the extreme nature of their dishonesty after they left. The mail that followed them was addressed to a multitude of names, including current utility bills. After contacting these companies, we discovered the issue and were so thankful they had moved out. This taught us to be more cautious when interviewing future prospective tenants, but it is not an exact science.

So you see, in today's day and age, you don't always get what you think you're getting. Though we use the basic standards, we must also try to prepare for the unexpected as best as we can by keeping our eyes open and tuned it to what is happening.

2

The Lease Agreement

We usually ask our prospective tenants to sign a one year lease, although some prefer a month-to-month agreement. Either option usually works for us as long as rent is paid in a timely manner. If someone does not pay rent, then they will not be staying for the rest of the year anyway. We are also flexible when tenants request an update to their payment schedule at the end of a lease agreement. For instance, if a tenant would like to switch from their annual agreement to a month-to-month once their initial agreement expires, we will definitely consider this option. Or, if they are on a month-to-month plan, are paying on time and would like to extend it for 6 more months, again we will most likely agree. We have found that typically the lease plan that best suits the tenant is indeed the one that will work for us.

We offer an alternative to help lower their monthly lease payment. This is available in the form of a work-share agreement. During the signing of the lease, we usually ask the tenant if they would like to save money each month on their rent starting immediately. What we do is offer them a $50.00 deduction from their rent if they agree to do all the minor repairs around the house, cut the lawn with the lawn mower and gas we provide, and in the winter time shovel the snow and keep the walkway clean. We include this in their lease agreement and to verify compliance, we frequently drive by our homes to ensure maintenance is being completed. If not, we approach our tenants and address the situation as needed, whether than means nullifying the work-share agreement, or following up with them to guarantee compliance.

Another tenant-friendly lease agreement that has worked well for us is to provide the tenants with a 5-day grace period on their rent payment. This is also included within their lease agreement. After the 5-day grace period, a $75.00 late fee applies if rent is not paid. As stated earlier, it is not easy to charge this late fee since late payments are usually due to a money problem with the tenant. Most of our houses are occupied by families with young children and $75.00 can mean the difference between food, a car payment or even future rent. However, at the same time it is important to set rules to ensure a late payment issue does not compound into anything more drastic or chronic. To that end, we definitely encourage our tenants to notify us if they foresee any potential issues regarding an upcoming rent payment so we can discuss alternative options, such as weekly payments for a short period of time.

It is important for us to have a respectful relationship with our tenants and in particular that they respect our house. We do not want to begin eviction proceedings with someone over a rent payment being 15 days late. We are not comfortable being that strict so quickly, and plus it is not always good business sense. However, if they can't pay or have no intention of paying, then that is a totally different program altogether.

With respect to other items within the lease agreement, we do allow pets as long as they clean up after them both inside the house and in the yard. Dogs must be kept in a fenced yard or on a leash if outside a fenced area. Our biggest worry is that the dog will bite or injure someone walking by or visiting the tenant and we become indirectly liable.

Trampolines are not allowed, but during the summer we may allow a tenant to purchase a little disposable pool for their children. If so, we require them to pay the water bill, ensure they have appropriate liability insurance and lock and close the gates to the yard at all times.

While we do not require that our tenants have renter's insurance, we do strongly recommend that they do so. For only a few hundred dollars a year they would have coverage for their items in the house in the event of fire or theft. Unfortunately, many simply cannot afford the payment or perhaps they just do not bother to do so, but it is something we discuss with them.

Obviously, drugs are absolutely prohibited as are all illegal activities. If we catch our tenants using or selling illegal drugs on our property, or engaging in any illegal activities, we notify the proper authorities, the lease is immediately terminated and they have to vacate. We openly discuss this during the application process along with the other issues.

We request that rent be paid by check or money order and sent to our business address. We prefer not to receive rent in cash. Not only is it dangerous to have that money in cash on one's person, but there is no formal record of the payment. We have, however, allowed this in extreme circumstances in the past.

All tenants living in the residence over age 18 must sign the lease agreement and are responsible for the rent payment unless those residents are children of the primary renters. We also need to know the names and ages of each one of the children that will be staying in the house, not only for liability reasons but for safety reasons. If an emergency situation were to arise, such as a fire, it is important to be aware of all of the people living in the household.

Another item listed in our lease is the requirement that a tenant notify us of a new phone number within 10 days. This is common courtesy, but is also necessary as we need to be able to reach our tenants for emergencies. Although we have had to place notes on our tenants' doors telling them that their phone numbers are disconnected and to contact us with their new number.

If for any reason a rent check is returned to us with insufficient funds from the bank, we charge an additional $50.00 plus the cost of the returned check, which is generally about $15.00.

The tenants are allowed and encouraged to fix and repair items in the house pursuant to the clause in the contract for a $50.00 reduction, but they are not allowed to do any improvements or alterations without our knowledge and approval. And in no way are any alterations and improvements done in lieu of their normal rent payments with us.

They are also not allowed to change the locks without our knowledge. If for any reason we need to change the locks or re-key them due to a tenant-generated issue, we will charge the full cost of the operation.

We absolutely do not enter the house nor do we allow any other person to enter the house without the tenant's authorization and permission. In the event we have no choice due to an emergency and we are not able to immediately locate the tenant, we leave messages and notes as applicable. No one enters without one of us there to keep control of the matter and to protect their contents.

The rest of the lease information is basic lease agreement language and details. We use a standard lease agreement that we received from a friend of ours, but you can get them online, you can make your own, or you can purchase them along with all other rental forms at Staples and Office Max.

Due to the various state requirements for lease agreements, we are not including a sample here. We do, however, suggest that you use the resources noted above to find examples of leases used within your state.

One final note here is what we do when a tenant moves in, which is a pre-lease house inspection. That way we all know and have agreed upon the exact condition of the house and all of the appliances. At the end of the lease, if there are any damages and we want to use some of the security deposit money to repair it, we have a form showing us the initial agreed upon condition of that item. For instance, one example is if a large hole is in a wall, we may deduct this from the security deposit if it is not identified during this inspection. On the other hand, this also allows us to see if any minor repairs, such as a leaky faucet, need to be repaired by us prior to the move-in. In sum, we have found this to be a quick, easy, and helpful start to our lease partnership. It shows the tenant that we are aware of the condition of everything and that we care about the condition of every item in the house. They also remember this every time they break or destroy something!

3

Difficult Tenants

As mentioned earlier, unfortunately there are tenants who simply will not or are not able to pay rent. This has already happened to us twice although we were able to get rid of the tenants with limited difficulty.

The first time, we had tenants who paid in cash which we weren't all that thrilled about for the reasons we have already stated. Initially, they seemed great but after about three months it spiraled downhill fast. They stopped answering the door when we came by to pick up the rent money. We could hear them inside whispering and it was frustrating because it was as though they were hiding inside our house, but we could not enter or do anything about it at that moment.

When the rent became 15 days past due in the final month, we sent them a rent due letter in the mail as well as posted a notice on their door. In the letter we gave them a timeline for the rent payment and if no money was received during that timeframe then we advised them that we would begin proceedings to have them vacate the property. Our letter looks very official as we print it on our corporate stationary and to add to its effectiveness we also include our corporate seal. Please see an example of this form in the Helpful Documents section.

In this case, the tenants moved out of the house prior to the timeline noted in our rent due letter. We found out afterwards that they also had an issue paying the utilities by the time we had posted the rent due notice, because the power had been already shut off. We're not certain why they left so quickly, but it was winter and thus very cold outside, so we believe they found another place to live with heat.

While their move-out was relatively pain-free to us, the post-move was not. They left an incredible mess throughout the house that just amazed us. There were flies, ants and garbage strewn all over the house, along with more pennies than we could count. They apparently did not like pennies very much as they were thrown around the house. If only they had more respect for money, perhaps they could have at least attempted to meet their financial obligations.

The next eviction followed a similar pattern except the tenants stopped paying almost immediately. Their power was initially in our name and one day we received a bill from the power company for $150.00. Not only were they not paying the rent, they never transferred the utilities over into their names. We immediately called the utility company and explained that we had a renter and that we needed the name transferred as soon as possible. A few nights later we went to the house to try and collect the rent again and to discuss the situation, but they wouldn't come to the door. We posted an Energy termination notice on the door as well as the rent due notice as we had with the previous renters.

Several days later we drove over to the house again to see what was going on and to try talking with them in person. The electricity had been shut off by the utility company as had the gas so there should have been no lights or anything. To our amazement, however, the outside lights were on as well as a few on the inside.

We knocked and knocked and no one answered. By this time, they should have been out, as the neighbors advised us that they saw them pack up a pickup truck the prior day. We decided that they were probably gone, so we entered the house cautiously.

Now these folks had been in the house for only 60 days and we still cannot believe how completely grimy and messy it was when they vacated. We simply do not know how a family with a young child can do so much damage to a house, let alone live in such total filth. Holes were punched in the walls, garbage and other unwanted junk was thrown throughout the entire house, and the carpet was completely destroyed. They had broken the oven door on our 6-month old stove, but perhaps the worst was the maggot infestation in the kitchen and refrigerator thanks to the food that was tossed in and around the sink. It was truly unbelievable.

This sounds like a horrible outcome, but we found the best thing to do was just roll up our sleeves, plug our noses and begin the cleanup. Fortunately, the house was relatively small so we were able to reverse a lot of the damage in just a few hours. In addition, as we said earlier we have a great handy man. He found a new oven at a garage sale for $15 and he did the wall and general repairs both inside and outside for under $1000, which including painting and re-building a back fence. In truth, the house actually ended up looking much better then when it was initially rented.

Naturally, we would have preferred that this did not happen, but we accepted it as part of our learning experience. We could have been stricter with our initial review of them as potential tenants, but it's hard to say if that would have prevented it entirely. What it has taught us is that there are people that do not live like we do and do not respect what we respect in life.

From our conversations with landlords, it appears that there is a good chance you will come across difficult tenants at some point. What you can do is determine your limits and prepare yourself as much as possible for situations such as this. For instance, the damage they caused is exactly why a security deposit is typically required. While this did not pay for the repairs entirely, it certainly helps minimize the costs. Furthermore, we were also willing to put our own time and energy into cleaning the place which helped us realize how far we were willing to go to try to make the house suitable to rent again.

Part VII
Conclusion

Conclusion

This is the end, but at the same time, this is just the beginning for us in our journey in investing in rental properties and real estate. We love to explore and we love to get in the car and look at houses and new communities and towns as you may, too.

We are always on the look out for that next big adventure. Maybe it's here in our new home state of Michigan or maybe it's in a new state. We won't know until we get out there and explore.

That's our advice to you. There are great deals out there everywhere. Some close to your home and some far away. The only way you will find them is by exploring the country, driving up and down streets, and investigating properties online. You have to be motivated to look around your neighborhood and beyond.

Perhaps when you're perusing local papers or just out of sheer chance you're driving down that new street on the other side of town, you will find it. You will find that one house that fits within your plan perfectly. Then once you close on that house and have a renter in place, you can start the process all over again.

Once you have that deal done, you can think about how to do your next deal or how to finance the next deal. Do you do a land contract, or traditional financing? Do you consider seller financing or do you take the equity out of your last purchase to leverage the next purchase?

We know of a couple who have over 100 rental houses and each year, they take equity out of a few of them and use that money to buy a couple new ones with cash. No loans.

By the time you close your first deal you will have been bitten by the bug and you will want another one fast. Just remember to stick to your plan, make the math work monthly and only buy when it is right. It's much better to say no to someone else's problems today, then it is to have that house and tenant as your new problem tomorrow.

There is money to be made in Real Estate investing, whether it is our plan of buy, rent and hold or the buy and flip-for-a-profit method. No way is a sure thing that is certain but when you buy for the long haul and plan properly you are more likely than not to succeed. Remember the old adage: when the time comes, buy low and sell high. Get the best possible deal you can today on the best possible property and your chances of selling high improve greatly.

In markets where you have a massive number of foreclosures there can be even more interesting ways to do a deal. In some cases you may find a seller who is late on their payments and backed up on taxes and the loan is with a local bank. In some cases, that bank may allow you to simply assume that seller's loan in an effort to avoid foreclosure. This allows the seller to get out from under a tremendous financial burden and provides you with a house with little if no money out of your pocket. It also makes that local bank very happy to have someone making those payments again and on time.

One way to find deals such as this is to market specifically for what you want. Go up to the houses of sellers and talk to them, or distribute flyers explaining exactly what you seek. Remember, you won't know what the seller is willing to negotiate unless you ask. Be confident, honest and direct and you will surely find the deal that fits your plan. And most importantly you must make sure that money works on any deal such as this. Don't just assume the sellers loan because it is easy, assume it because it is the right deal.

Finally, take your time when buying houses. Don't rush to acquire as many houses as you can in as short a time as possible. That is how many mistakes are made. Take your time, learn the business and do it right as best as you can. You will make some mistakes and you will need to recover from them. Most of the time, these mistakes will cost you money, but that is oftentimes how you will best learn what to do the next time around. So don't over-extend yourself financially and be prepared for any occurrences.

Good luck and have fun!

Helpful Documents

NOTICE OF TERMINATION OF LEASE

To: _____

Regarding property located at

_____

This notice is to give you notice that pursuant to the provisions of our lease agreement, you are in violation of items #_____ #_____ #_____

As of this date_____, I have elected to terminate your lease and will file Eviction papers on _____

With the City of_____

You have an opportunity to vacate the premises as of

_____.

And we will not take any further action. However, all security deposit money will be forfeited by you.

Please sign this form and leave it in the kitchen in a visible place upon your exit from the house on _____ date.

If you are still in the residence as of _____date, then we will assume you have elected to be evicted by the courts and we will proceed as such.

_____

(Landlord's name and title here)

Place corporate seal/stamp here

ENERGY TERMINATION NOTICE

To: _____

Address:_____

From: _____

RE: Termination of utility services in landlord's name.

As of _____date, tenant _____has failed to transfer the household utilities at address_____ into their name.

Therefore, as of _____date, I have notified the Utility Company, _____, that the service is to be cancelled in my name.

You have _____ days to contact the utility company and have the service placed in your name, or risk being without power.

To that, as the tenant and pursuant to our lease agreement, any damages done to the house as a result of loss of power is the financial responsibility of the tenant. As an example: burst pipes or fire damage.

You are required to keep the house in proper working order and in good condition. You can and will be held liable for any and all problems that could arise as a result of this negligence.

_____
(Landlord's name and title here)

Place your corporate seal/stamp here

PRE-LEASE INSPECTION REPORT

Date of inspection_____   Date of move in_____

Living room condition
Great_____   Good_____   Poor_____
List any concerns or faults_____

Kitchen condition
Great_____   Good_____   Poor_____
List any concerns or faults_____

Bedroom 1
Great_____   Good_____   Poor_____
List any concerns or faults_____

Bedroom II
Great_____   Good_____   Poor_____
List any concerns or faults_____

Bedroom III
Great_____   Good_____   Poor_____
List any concerns or faults_____

Other room _____
Great_____   Good_____   Poor_____
List any concerns or faults_____

Exterior of house, list any concerns, defects or faults
_____

Other_____

_____   _____
Tenant's initials   Landlord's initials

Property address:_____

POST-LEASE INSPECTION REPORT

Date of final inspection_____   Date of tenant's departure_____

Living room condition
Great_____   Good_____   Poor_____ PASS/FAIL_____
List any concerns or faults_____

Kitchen condition
Great_____   Good_____   Poor_____   PASS/FAIL_____
List any concerns or faults_____

Bedroom 1
Great_____   Good_____   Poor_____   PASS/FAIL_____
List any concerns or faults_____

Bedroom II
Great_____   Good_____   Poor_____   PASS/FAIL_____
List any concerns or faults_____

Bedroom III
Great_____   Good_____   Poor_____   PASS/FAIL_____
List any concerns or faults_____

Other room _____   PASS/FAIL_____
Great_____   Good_____   Poor_____

List any concerns or faults_____

Exterior of house, list any concerns, defects or faults
_____
Other_____

_____   _____
Tenant's initials   Landlord's initials

Property address_____

NOTICE OF RENT DUE

This notice, in pursuant to the dated Rental contract, _____,
between _____and landlord/property owner, _____.

In so far as the tenant is required to pay rent on time or provide proper notification to landlord of such tardiness. The tenant _____ has not properly executed pursuant to the rental contract.

As of this notice, there has/have been _____ times where rent was late or short. On these dates_____. Each time a late fee has been assessed of $75 dollars. Each time the late fee (circle one) **has or has not** been paid by the tenant.

This is to serve notice that the rent is due immediately in the amount of_____ Which includes $_____ which is _____

Due to the habitual lateness of rent, starting on _____, rent is due in its entirety on the 1st of the month for $_____.

Once tenant has successfully attained 6 straight months of on-time payments, the landlord/property owner will revert the payment plan back to once every 2 weeks.

Currently, rent is due for a total of $_____ immediately!

If tenant is planning on vacating the house, notice is due immediately. If rent is not received within 24 hours, termination of lease between lessor and lessee is immediate due to breach of contract and tenant forfeits all earnest deposit money.

_____
(Landlord name here and title)

978-0-595-46638-2
0-595-46638-9

www.ingramcontent.com/pod-product-compliance
Lightning Source LLC
Chambersburg PA
CBHW021007180526
45163CB00005B/1926